Adult

MAD LIBS®

The world's greatest *food and wine* game

Eat, Drink, and Be Mad Libs

by Douglas Yacka

Mad Libs
An Imprint of Penguin Random House

MAD LIBS
An Imprint of Penguin Random House LLC

Concept created by Roger Price & Leonard Stern

Published by Mad Libs,
an imprint of Penguin Random House LLC,
345 Hudson Street, New York, New York 10014.
Printed in the USA.

ISBN 9780843180718
3 5 7 9 10 8 6 4

Adult MAD LIBS® INSTRUCTIONS

The world's greatest _food and wine_ game

MAD LIBS® is a game for people who don't like games!
It can be played by one, two, three, four, or forty.

• RIDICULOUSLY SIMPLE DIRECTIONS

In this book, you'll find stories containing blank spaces where words are left out. One player, the READER, selects one of the stories. The READER shouldn't tell anyone what the story is about. Instead, the READER should ask the other players, the WRITERS, to give words to fill in the blank spaces in the story.

• TO PLAY

The READER asks each WRITER in turn to call out words—adjectives or nouns or whatever the spaces call for—and uses them to fill in the blank spaces in the story. The result is your very own MAD LIBS! Then, when the READER reads the completed MAD LIBS to the other players, they will discover they have written a story that is fantastic, screamingly funny, shocking, silly, crazy, or just plain dumb—depending on the words each WRITER called out.

• EXAMPLE (*Before* and *After*)

" _____ !" he said _____
            EXCLAMATION   ADVERB

as he jumped into his convertible _____ and
                                              NOUN

drove off with his _____ wife.
                              ADJECTIVE

" _____*Ouch*_____ !" he said _____*stupidly*_____
            EXCLAMATION   ADVERB

as he jumped into his convertible _____*cat*_____ and
                                              NOUN

drove off with his _____*brave*_____ wife.
                              ADJECTIVE

In case you have forgotten what adjectives, adverbs, nouns, and verbs are, here is a quick review:

An **ADJECTIVE** describes something or somebody. *Lumpy, soft, ugly, messy,* and *short* are adjectives.

An **ADVERB** tells how something is done. It modifies a verb and usually ends in "ly." *Modestly, stupidly, greedily,* and *carefully* are adverbs.

A **NOUN** is the name of a person, place, or thing. *Sidewalk, umbrella, bridle, bathtub,* and *nose* are nouns.

A **VERB** is an action word. *Run, pitch, jump,* and *swim* are verbs. Put the verbs in past tense if the directions say **PAST TENSE**. *Ran, pitched, jumped,* and *swam* are verbs in the past tense.

When we ask for **A PLACE**, we mean any sort of place: a country or city (*Spain, Cleveland*) or a room (*bathroom, kitchen*).

An **EXCLAMATION** or **SILLY WORD** is any sort of funny sound, gasp, grunt, or outcry, like *Wow!, Ouch!, Whomp!, Ick!,* and *Gadzooks!*

When we ask for specific words, like a **NUMBER**, a **COLOR**, an **ANIMAL**, or a **PART OF THE BODY**, we mean a word that is one of those things, like *seven, blue, horse,* or *head*.

When we ask for a **PLURAL**, it means more than one. For example, *cat* pluralized is *cats*.

MAD LIBS® is fun to play with friends, but you can also play it by yourself! To begin with, DO NOT look at the story on the page below. Fill in the blanks on this page with the words called for. Then, using the words you have selected, fill in the blank spaces in the story. Now you've created your own hilarious MAD LIBS® game!

NOUN _____

VERB ENDING IN "ING" _____

NOUN _____

ADJECTIVE _____

PART OF THE BODY _____

ADJECTIVE _____

ADJECTIVE _____

NOUN _____

PLURAL NOUN _____

ADVERB _____

PART OF THE BODY _____

NOUN _____

ADJECTIVE _____

PLURAL NOUN _____

TYPE OF EVENT _____

NOUN _____

Adult MAD LIBS® WINE TASTING 101

The world's greatest _food and wine_ game

As any connoisseur will tell you, appreciating a/an _____ of
                                                      NOUN

wine is like _____ a fine work of art.
              VERB ENDING IN "ING"

First, you must hold up your glass to examine the color. Does

the shade remind you of a/an _____? Is the wine light or
                                 NOUN

_____-bodied? Next, put your _____ into the glass
  ADJECTIVE   PART OF THE BODY

and sniff. Is the aroma _____, or is it more _____?
                            ADJECTIVE   ADJECTIVE

You might detect a hint of _____. You might even smell
                               NOUN

_____. Once you have done this, you should _____
  PLURAL NOUN   ADVERB

take a sip. Make sure you swish it around your _____ before
                                                   PART OF THE BODY

swallowing. Is that _____ you taste? Is the wine _____
                        NOUN   ADJECTIVE

or dry? Congratulations! Now you can impress your _____
                                                       PLURAL NOUN

the next time you attend a/an _____. And don't forget to raise
                                  TYPE OF EVENT

your glass and give the classic toast, "To your _____!"
                                                    NOUN

Adult
MAD LIBS® RESTAURANT REVIEW

The world's greatest _food and wine_ game

MAD LIBS® is fun to play with friends, but you can also play it by yourself! To begin with, DO NOT look at the story on the page below. Fill in the blanks on this page with the words called for. Then, using the words you have selected, fill in the blank spaces in the story. Now you've created your own hilarious MAD LIBS® game!

CITY _____

ADJECTIVE _____

NOUN _____

ADVERB _____

OCCUPATION _____

ADJECTIVE _____

NOUN _____

TYPE OF FOOD _____

ADJECTIVE _____

VERB _____

ANIMAL _____

ADJECTIVE _____

NOUN _____

PERSON IN ROOM _____

TYPE OF LIQUID _____

NOUN _____

ADJECTIVE _____

NUMBER _____

The _____ _Herald_'s review of the _____
CITY   ADJECTIVE

_____ Café, our city's hottest new restaurant:
NOUN

"I can _____ say that in all of my years as a/an
ADVERB

_____, I have never encountered such a/an _____
OCCUPATION   ADJECTIVE

establishment. You may choose to begin your meal with a salad of

arugula and _____, although I much preferred the cream
NOUN

of _____ soup. Portions are _____, so you should
TYPE OF FOOD   ADJECTIVE

plan to _____ for several minutes before moving to
VERB

entrées. I selected the rack of _____, which was especially
ANIMAL

_____ due to the unexpected addition of _____
ADJECTIVE   NOUN

to the seasoning. Other options included steak à la _____
PERSON IN ROOM

and salmon with _____ sauce. The house specialty dessert
TYPE OF LIQUID

is a frosted layer cake, which I recommend that you order with a

scoop of _____ cream. Overall, this is one _____
NOUN   ADJECTIVE

destination. I give it _____ stars!"
NUMBER

Adult MAD LIBS® BLOOPER MARKET

The world's greatest _food and wine_ game

MAD LIBS® is fun to play with friends, but you can also play it by yourself! To begin with, DO NOT look at the story on the page below. Fill in the blanks on this page with the words called for. Then, using the words you have selected, fill in the blank spaces in the story. Now you've created your own hilarious MAD LIBS® game!

ANIMAL _____

NOUN _____

ADJECTIVE _____

NUMBER _____

COLOR _____

VERB ENDING "ING" _____

TYPE OF LIQUID _____

EXCLAMATION _____

SILLY WORD _____

FIRST NAME (MALE) _____

PLURAL NOUN _____

ADJECTIVE _____

ANIMAL _____

VERB _____

NOUN _____

PERSON IN ROOM _____

VERB ENDING IN "ING" _____

Adult MAD LIBS® BLOOPER MARKET

The world's greatest _food and wine_ game

Good morning, honey-_____,

ANIMAL

Can you please swing by the supermarket today and pick up a few

things? We need:

• A fresh _____-melon. Make sure to squeeze it first to see if

NOUN

it's _____.

ADJECTIVE

• _____ _____ apples; the kind you use for

NUMBER   COLOR

_____.

VERB ENDING IN "ING"

• One carton of _____. Don't forget to check the expiration date.

TYPE OF LIQUID

_____—we don't want a repeat of what happened last time!

EXCLAMATION

• A large box of _____-Os; the one with a picture of

SILLY WORD

_____ the Tiger on the front.

FIRST NAME (MALE)

• A dozen _____. Make sure their shells aren't broken.

PLURAL NOUN

• Two packages of _____-range _____ breasts.

ADJECTIVE   ANIMAL

• And don't forget to _____ at the deli counter. We need

VERB

sliced _____ for little _____'s lunch.

NOUN   PERSON IN ROOM

When you get home, the cleaning and _____ lists are on the

VERB ENDING IN "ING"

fridge. Enjoy your day off!

Adult MAD LIBS MANGIA! MANGIA! MANGIA!

The world's greatest _food and wine_ game

MAD LIBS® is fun to play with friends, but you can also play it by yourself! To begin with, DO NOT look at the story on the page below. Fill in the blanks on this page with the words called for. Then, using the words you have selected, fill in the blank spaces in the story. Now you've created your own hilarious MAD LIBS® game!

NOUN _____

ADJECTIVE _____

NUMBER _____

PART OF THE BODY (PLURAL) _____

COLOR _____

NOUN _____

VERB (PAST TENSE) _____

PERSON IN ROOM (MALE) _____

NOUN _____

ANIMAL _____

ANIMAL _____

ADVERB _____

ADJECTIVE _____

TYPE OF LIQUID _____

EXCLAMATION _____

Every Sunday, rain or _____, my Italian grandma, or

NOUN

Nonna, as we called her, would cook a/an _____ feast.

ADJECTIVE

By _____ o'clock, the entire family would be licking their

NUMBER

_____ in anticipation. Early in the day, Nonna began her

PART OF THE BODY (PLURAL)

_____ sauce. None of us knew for sure, but Dad used to tell

COLOR

us that a sprinkle of _____ and a dash of oregano were her

NOUN

secrets to the seasoning. The pasta was more controversial. Nonna

checked if it was finished by holding it in her hand and watching

how it _____. But our uncle, ' _____ the Knuckle,'

VERB PAST TENSE   PERSON IN ROOM (MALE)

would throw a few noodles against the _____ to see if they

NOUN

stuck. One thing we all agreed on was Nonna's meatballs. She mixed

_____ and veal together with a little _____ thrown in

ANIMAL   ANIMAL

for good luck. She _____ handcrafted each ball to create the

ADVERB

most _____ thing we'd ever tasted. And before we ate, Nonna

ADJECTIVE

would pour a glass of _____ and exclaim—" _____!"

TYPE OF LIQUID   EXCLAMATION

Adult MAD LIBS® RAW COURAGE

The world's greatest _food and wine_ game

MAD LIBS® is fun to play with friends, but you can also play it by yourself! To begin with, DO NOT look at the story on the page below. Fill in the blanks on this page with the words called for. Then, using the words you have selected, fill in the blank spaces in the story. Now you've created your own hilarious MAD LIBS® game!

ANIMAL _____

PLURAL NOUN _____

NUMBER _____

PART OF THE BODY _____

VERB ENDING IN "ING" _____

NOUN _____

VERB ENDING IN "ING" _____

NOUN _____

ADJECTIVE _____

NOUN _____

ADJECTIVE _____

ANIMAL _____

ADJECTIVE _____

VERB ENDING IN "ING" _____

NUMBER _____

While many are afraid of eating uncooked _____, it is
ANIMAL

actually quite delicious. _____ have been enjoying sushi for
PLURAL NOUN

at least _____ centuries. Before eating sushi, you must first
NUMBER

master the chopsticks. Hold them firmly in your _____ and
PART OF THE BODY

practice opening and _____ them. When you are able to pick
VERB ENDING IN "ING"

up a grain of _____, you have truly mastered this technique.
NOUN

Finally it's time to eat. If this is your first time, try _____
VERB ENDING IN "ING"

the vegetable roll to start, or the _____ tempura. Feeling
NOUN

_____? Good. It's time to move on. Spicy _____ is
ADJECTIVE NOUN

a favorite, as well as the _____ eel, sometimes referred to as
ADJECTIVE

the _____ of the sea. If you're feeling especially adventurous,
ANIMAL

order the _____ clam. Just beware of the blowfish. It can be
ADJECTIVE

poisonous, and might leave you _____ in the hospital for
VERB ENDING IN "ING"

_____ days!
NUMBER

MAD LIBS® is fun to play with friends, but you can also play it by yourself! To begin with, DO NOT look at the story on the page below. Fill in the blanks on this page with the words called for. Then, using the words you have selected, fill in the blank spaces in the story. Now you've created your own hilarious MAD LIBS® game!

NUMBER _____

PLURAL NOUN _____

FIRST NAME (MALE) _____

PLURAL NOUN _____

TYPE OF LIQUID _____

CELEBRITY _____

ADVERB _____

PLURAL NOUN _____

A PLACE _____

ADJECTIVE _____

VERB ENDING IN "ING" _____

ADJECTIVE _____

PLURAL NOUN _____

PART OF THE BODY (PLURAL) _____

ADJECTIVE _____

VERB ENDING IN "ING" _____

The history of wine began nearly _____ years ago, when
NUMBER

people all over the world discovered that getting drunk was more fun

than building statues of _____. The Romans, under Emperor
PLURAL NOUN

_____, traded barrels for _____. The Greeks made
FIRST NAME (MALE) PLURAL NOUN

_____ in honor of _____, the goddess of wine.
TYPE OF LIQUID CELEBRITY

During the Middle Ages, peasants worked _____ to supply
ADVERB

noble _____ and queens with their beverage of choice. If
PLURAL NOUN

the wine wasn't acceptable, they were exiled to (the) _____.
A PLACE

France became well-known for the _____ wines of
ADJECTIVE

Bordeaux. Emperor Napoleon Bonaparte is said to have celebrated

by _____ wine after every victory. In Italy, _____
VERB ENDING IN "ING" ADJECTIVE

vineyards covered the _____ of the countryside. It was there
PLURAL NOUN

that the tradition of crushing grapes with one's _____
PART OF THE BODY (PLURAL)

originated. Today, many of the most _____ wines are made
ADJECTIVE

in the USA. California is the best place to find them. So when you're

done _____ your surfboard, kick back and pour yourself a
VERB ENDING IN "ING"

glass, dude!

Adult MAD LIBS

INQUIRE WITHIN

The world's greatest _food and wine_ game

MAD LIBS® is fun to play with friends, but you can also play it by yourself! To begin with, DO NOT look at the story on the page below. Fill in the blanks on this page with the words called for. Then, using the words you have selected, fill in the blank spaces in the story. Now you've created your own hilarious MAD LIBS® game!

ADJECTIVE _____

NUMBER _____

OCCUPATION _____

VERB ENDING IN "ING" _____

ADVERB _____

PLURAL NOUN _____

PLURAL NOUN _____

NOUN _____

TYPE OF LIQUID _____

ADJECTIVE _____

VERB _____

ADJECTIVE _____

PART OF THE BODY _____

NOUN _____

PLURAL NOUN _____

Busy café is seeking a/an _____ waiter or waitress.
ADJECTIVE

_____ years of experience is required, and previous
NUMBER

employment as a/an _____ is a plus. The ideal worker will be
OCCUPATION

great at _____ for long periods of time, and be able to move
VERB ENDING IN "ING"

_____ in a crowded area. A strong working knowledge of
ADVERB

_____ and _____ is preferred. He or she should know
PLURAL NOUN   PLURAL NOUN

how to carry a/an _____ and pour a glass of _____.
NOUN   TYPE OF LIQUID

Must be extremely _____ and willing to _____ on
ADJECTIVE   VERB

weekends and holidays. A/An _____ demeanor is essential—
ADJECTIVE

you should always have a smile on your _____. This is an
PART OF THE BODY

opportunity to make a/an _____-load of money. Only serious
NOUN

_____ need apply.
PLURAL NOUN

Adult MAD LIBS® EAT YOUR HEART OUT

The world's greatest *food and wine* game

MAD LIBS® is fun to play with friends, but you can also play it by yourself! To begin with, DO NOT look at the story on the page below. Fill in the blanks on this page with the words called for. Then, using the words you have selected, fill in the blank spaces in the story. Now you've created your own hilarious MAD LIBS® game!

ADJECTIVE _____

ADJECTIVE _____

ADJECTIVE _____

PLURAL NOUN _____

ADJECTIVE _____

OCCUPATION (PLURAL) _____

ANIMAL _____

ADJECTIVE _____

VERB _____

TYPE OF LIQUID _____

NOUN _____

NOUN _____

VERB ENDING IN "ING" _____

TYPE OF FOOD _____

PART OF THE BODY (PLURAL) _____

VERB _____

Adult MAD LIBS® EAT YOUR HEART OUT

The world's greatest _food and wine_ game

Do you and your sweetheart wish to rekindle the _____

ADJECTIVE

romance in your relationship? You may not realize it, but it's possible

to rediscover the magic with the help of some familiar foods. Oysters

are the most _____ and well-known aphrodisiac. They are

ADJECTIVE

high in minerals that are said to put you in a/an _____

ADJECTIVE

mood. Pomegranate juice is another favorite for frisky _____.

PLURAL NOUN

Figs have a/an _____ reputation as well. It is rumored that

ADJECTIVE

Cleopatra had her _____ feed them to her in bed. You could

OCCUPATION (PLURAL)

try feasting on _____ in order to bring out the beast in the

ANIMAL

bedroom! And, of course, don't forget the _____ chocolate.

ADJECTIVE

But don't feel that you have to limit yourself to these— _____

VERB

your imagination! Strawberries, whipped _____, and

TYPE OF LIQUID

_____ butter are some _____ staples that make a great

NOUN   NOUN

addition to a night of love- _____. We've even heard of lovers

VERB ENDING IN "ING"

putting _____ on their _____! And if none of

TYPE OF FOOD   PART OF THE BODY (PLURAL)

these work, you can always _____ a bottle of vodka and hope

VERB

for the best!

MAD LIBS® is fun to play with friends, but you can also play it by yourself! To begin with, DO NOT look at the story on the page below. Fill in the blanks on this page with the words called for. Then, using the words you have selected, fill in the blank spaces in the story. Now you've created your own hilarious MAD LIBS® game!

NOUN _____

VERB ENDING IN "ING" _____

ANIMAL (PLURAL) _____

PLURAL NOUN _____

VERB _____

NOUN _____

VERB _____

TYPE OF FOOD _____

PLURAL NOUN _____

TYPE OF LIQUID _____

VERB _____

EXCLAMATION _____

ADJECTIVE _____

A PLACE _____

Adult MAD LIBS® MISS MANNERS ANSWERS YOUR QUESTIONS

The world's greatest _food and wine_ game

Q: Dear Miss Manners, every time I go to a/an _____ party, I

NOUN

embarrass myself by _____ in front of the other guests. How

VERB ENDING IN "ING"

do I deal with this embarrassing problem?

MM: Dear reader, it sounds like a case of _____ in your

ANIMAL (PLURAL)

stomach. Try picturing your fellow party-goers without their

_____. This should help you to _____ and enjoy the evening.

PLURAL NOUN   VERB

Q: On a recent stay with friends, I arrived without a/an

_____ for the hosts. Should I have brought a gift to say

NOUN

" _____ you" for their hospitality?

VERB

MM: Traditionally, freshly baked _____ is given, but you also

TYPE OF FOOD

could present them with a bouquet of _____ or a bottle of

PLURAL NOUN

_____ as a way of saying "thanks."

TYPE OF LIQUID

Q: My husband and I are in the middle of a disagreement. Is it okay

to _____ at the dinner table?

VERB

MM: _____! I have never heard of anything so

EXCLAMATION

_____. I suggest that you move to (the) _____, where

ADJECTIVE   A PLACE

such behavior is considered acceptable.

Adult
MAD LIBS® TONIGHT ON FOOD TV

The world's greatest *food and wine* game

MAD LIBS® is fun to play with friends, but you can also play it by yourself! To begin with, DO NOT look at the story on the page below. Fill in the blanks on this page with the words called for. Then, using the words you have selected, fill in the blank spaces in the story. Now you've created your own hilarious MAD LIBS® game!

OCCUPATION (PLURAL) _____

PERSON IN ROOM _____

NUMBER _____

COLOR _____

NOUN _____

VEHICLE _____

CELEBRITY _____

CELEBRITY _____

ADJECTIVE _____

PLURAL NOUN _____

TYPE OF LIQUID _____

ANIMAL _____

ADJECTIVE _____

NOUN _____

VERB _____

PART OF THE BODY _____

ADJECTIVE _____

EXCLAMATION _____

Adult MAD LIBS

TONIGHT ON FOOD TV

The world's greatest _food and wine_ game

First up, our newest hit show, _____ *in the Kitchen*,
OCCUPATION (PLURAL)

hosted by Food TV's own Chef _____ McCheferson.
PERSON IN ROOM

In the series pilot, our host challenges amateur cooks to create

a/an _____-course meal, using only _____ eggs and
NUMBER   COLOR

_____ meat.
NOUN

And then, don't miss *Cupcake* _____. Join _____ and
VEHICLE   CELEBRITY

_____ as they travel the country in search of _____
CELEBRITY   ADJECTIVE

sweets and scrumptious _____.
PLURAL NOUN

Next, discover your adventurous side when we serve up

_____-glazed _____ sliders, on *Maniac Meals*. Are you
TYPE OF LIQUID   ANIMAL

_____ enough to ask what's for dinner?
ADJECTIVE

And finally, stay tuned for *The Ultimate* _____ *Cook-*
NOUN

off. Watch as your favorite Food TV stars _____ face-
VERB

to-_____ in a/an _____ battle of culinary skills.
PART OF THE BODY   ADJECTIVE

Chefs, get ready, set, _____!
EXCLAMATION

MAD LIBS® is fun to play with friends, but you can also play it by yourself! To begin with, DO NOT look at the story on the page below. Fill in the blanks on this page with the words called for. Then, using the words you have selected, fill in the blank spaces in the story. Now you've created your own hilarious MAD LIBS® game!

PLURAL NOUN _____

ADJECTIVE _____

TYPE OF LIQUID _____

ADJECTIVE _____

NOUN _____

VERB _____

ADJECTIVE _____

VERB (PAST TENSE) _____

CELEBRITY _____

CELEBRITY _____

ADJECTIVE _____

SILLY WORD _____

VERB _____

PERSON IN ROOM (MALE) _____

ADJECTIVE _____

PLURAL NOUN _____

ADJECTIVE _____

PERSON IN ROOM (MALE) _____

We here at Frosty World are excited to unveil our newest ice creams and frozen ＿＿＿＿＿＿.

PLURAL NOUN

This year we're mixing up some ＿＿＿＿＿＿ takes on classic flavors. Cookies & ＿＿＿＿＿＿,

ADJECTIVE ／ TYPE OF LIQUID

anyone? Perhaps Mocha Swirl or ＿＿＿＿＿＿ Vanilla might be

ADJECTIVE

more to your liking. Our personal favorite is Mint ＿＿＿＿＿＿

NOUN

Chip. The health-conscious can ＿＿＿＿＿＿ without the guilt while

VERB

enjoying one of our fruit sorbets or fat-free ＿＿＿＿＿＿ yogurts.

ADJECTIVE

They simply have to be ＿＿＿＿＿＿ to be believed. We're most

VERB (PAST TENSE)

excited about our Fame & Frosty lineup, featuring celebrity-inspired

ice-cream flavors such as ＿＿＿＿＿＿'s Rocky Road and Chocolate

CELEBRITY

Chip ＿＿＿＿＿＿ Dough. Music lovers will be ＿＿＿＿＿＿ for

CELEBRITY ／ ADJECTIVE

Lady ＿＿＿＿＿＿ Lemon, and classic rockers will ＿＿＿＿＿＿ for

SILLY WORD ／ VERB

＿＿＿＿＿＿ Springsteen's Dancing in the Dark Chocolate. Top our

PERSON IN ROOM (MALE)

＿＿＿＿＿＿ frozen treats off with some sprinkles, ＿＿＿＿＿＿, or

ADJECTIVE ／ PLURAL NOUN

＿＿＿＿＿＿ fudge and enjoy. You'll never go back to ＿＿＿＿＿＿

ADJECTIVE ／ PERSON IN ROOM (MALE)

& Jerry's!

Adult MAD LIBS® #FOODIEDILEMMAS

The world's greatest _food and wine_ game

MAD LIBS® is fun to play with friends, but you can also play it by yourself! To begin with, DO NOT look at the story on the page below. Fill in the blanks on this page with the words called for. Then, using the words you have selected, fill in the blank spaces in the story. Now you've created your own hilarious MAD LIBS® game!

A PLACE _____

VERB _____

PLURAL NOUN _____

VERB ENDING IN "ING" _____

NOUN _____

ANIMAL _____

A PLACE _____

PLURAL NOUN _____

OCCUPATION _____

OCCUPATION (PLURAL) _____

ADJECTIVE _____

VERB _____

NOUN _____

VERB _____

PLURAL NOUN _____

TYPE OF LIQUID _____

A text exchange between dining trenders, Brook and Lynn.

Brook: You around tonight? I was thinking we could check out that

new (the) _____ Supper Club. We need to _____
                A PLACE   VERB

early, though, because they only let in a few _____ each night.
                                                        PLURAL NOUN

Lynn: I'm _____ at the co-op until eight. Can we do the
              VERB ENDING IN "ING"

_____ Shack instead? I'm craving a lobster roll.
    NOUN

Brook: Totes over them, but _____ rolls are totally hot right now.
                                    ANIMAL

Lynn: How about Farm to _____ Bistro? It's super-local. They
                                A PLACE

even grow their own _____ and veggies on the roof, and you
                          PLURAL NOUN

can pick them yourself before the _____ prepares your meal.
                                        OCCUPATION

Brook: I hear their bartenders dress like old _____ with
                                                    OCCUPATION (PLURAL)

_____ little mustaches and suspenders. Pass!
    ADJECTIVE

Lynn: If we're really lucky, we can _____ at the pop-up
                                            VERB

restaurant in the basement of the _____ building downtown.
                                        NOUN

Brook: What if we just _____ at home and order a pizza?
                              VERB

Lynn: That's perfect. Now, what toppings? I like oven-roasted

_____ with a drizzle of locally harvested _____.
    PLURAL NOUN   TYPE OF LIQUID

MAD LIBS® is fun to play with friends, but you can also play it by yourself! To begin with, DO NOT look at the story on the page below. Fill in the blanks on this page with the words called for. Then, using the words you have selected, fill in the blank spaces in the story. Now you've created your own hilarious MAD LIBS® game!

ADJECTIVE _____

NOUN _____

OCCUPATION (PLURAL) _____

NUMBER _____

ADJECTIVE _____

TYPE OF LIQUID _____

NUMBER _____

SILLY WORD _____

TYPE OF FOOD _____

NOUN _____

TYPE OF LIQUID _____

ADJECTIVE _____

NUMBER _____

ADJECTIVE _____

SILLY WORD _____

ADJECTIVE _____

NOUN _____

Adult MAD LIBS®

THE JIVE OF JAVA

The world's greatest _food and wine_ game

These days, ordering coffee can be as _____ as buying a
                                        ADJECTIVE

new _____. Employees at the coffee shop are called
        NOUN

_____, so please address them as such. They will ask you
OCCUPATION (PLURAL)

which of the _____ beverage sizes you would like. Make sure
              NUMBER

to specify if you would prefer your coffee hot or _____. But
                                                   ADJECTIVE

many decisions remain . . .

- _____ instead of milk?
  TYPE OF LIQUID

- Replace sugar with one of _____ alternatives, including a
                            NUMBER

  packet of _____ sweetener, _____ syrup or a little
            SILLY WORD   TYPE OF FOOD

  whipped _____ on top?
          NOUN

- Order Japanese slow-drip brew instead of the usual, which pours

  _____ over the beans? Sounds _____, but do you
  TYPE OF LIQUID   ADJECTIVE

  have _____ minutes to stand around waiting for it? You're
       NUMBER

  not getting any younger here!

Still feeling lost? Then order our favorite: an extra-_____ soy
                                                      ADJECTIVE

_____ with two shots of _____-roasted espresso and a
SILLY WORD   ADJECTIVE

dash of _____.
        NOUN

MAD LIBS® is fun to play with friends, but you can also play it by yourself! To begin with, DO NOT look at the story on the page below. Fill in the blanks on this page with the words called for. Then, using the words you have selected, fill in the blank spaces in the story. Now you've created your own hilarious MAD LIBS® game!

PART OF THE BODY _____

ADJECTIVE _____

VERB _____

TYPE OF FOOD _____

ADJECTIVE _____

TYPE OF LIQUID _____

NOUN _____

ADJECTIVE _____

A PLACE _____

VERB ENDING IN "ING" _____

NOUN _____

OCCUPATION (PLURAL) _____

NOUN _____

PART OF THE BODY _____

Ever notice how many of our everyday expressions relate to food and drink? Here are some of our favorite bites of wisdom:

- You're the apple of my _____.
  PART OF THE BODY

- He's as _____ as a cucumber.
  ADJECTIVE

- I bit off more than I can _____.
  VERB

- You can't have your _____ and eat it, too.
  TYPE OF FOOD

- She dropped him like a/an _____ potato.
  ADJECTIVE

- They were full of the _____ of human kindness.
  TYPE OF LIQUID

- He was born with a silver _____ in his mouth.
  NOUN

- It's as _____ as molasses in January.
  ADJECTIVE

- Not for all the tea in (the) _____.
  A PLACE

- I feel like I'm _____ on eggshells.
  VERB ENDING IN "ING"

- Half a/an _____ is better than none.
  NOUN

- Too many _____ spoil the broth.
  OCCUPATION (PLURAL)

- Out of the frying pan, into the _____.
  NOUN

- Don't bite the _____ that feeds you.
  PART OF THE BODY

Adult MAD LIBS® FOOD FOR THOUGHT (PART 2)

The world's greatest *food and wine* game

MAD LIBS® is fun to play with friends, but you can also play it by yourself! To begin with, DO NOT look at the story on the page below. Fill in the blanks on this page with the words called for. Then, using the words you have selected, fill in the blank spaces in the story. Now you've created your own hilarious MAD LIBS® game!

ADJECTIVE _____

TYPE OF FOOD _____

ADJECTIVE _____

ANIMAL _____

PART OF THE BODY _____

PLURAL NOUN _____

TYPE OF LIQUID _____

NOUN _____

PLURAL NOUN _____

PLURAL NOUN _____

PART OF THE BODY (PLURAL) _____

NOUN _____

TYPE OF FOOD (PLURAL) _____

VERB _____

PLURAL NOUN _____

Here are some more _____ maxims from the kitchen:
ADJECTIVE

• It's the greatest thing since sliced _____.
TYPE OF FOOD

• What's _____ for the goose is good for the _____.
ADJECTIVE   ANIMAL

• The way to a man's heart is through his _____.
PART OF THE BODY

• They're just like two _____ in a pod.
PLURAL NOUN

• Don't cry over spilled _____.
TYPE OF LIQUID

• The fog is as thick as _____ soup.
NOUN

• You can't make an omelet without breaking some _____.
PLURAL NOUN

• I have bigger _____ to fry.
PLURAL NOUN

• He was caught with his _____ in the pie.
PART OF THE BODY (PLURAL)

• A watched _____ never boils.
NOUN

• It's not worth a hill of _____.
TYPE OF FOOD (PLURAL)

• I'm in a hurry; sorry to _____ and run.
VERB

• Life is like a box of _____. You never know what you're
PLURAL NOUN

gonna get.

MAD LIBS® is fun to play with friends, but you can also play it by yourself! To begin with, DO NOT look at the story on the page below. Fill in the blanks on this page with the words called for. Then, using the words you have selected, fill in the blank spaces in the story. Now you've created your own hilarious MAD LIBS® game!

ADJECTIVE _____

PLURAL NOUN _____

OCCUPATION _____

ADVERB _____

ADJECTIVE _____

PLURAL NOUN _____

NOUN _____

NOUN _____

TYPE OF FOOD _____

VERB _____

PERSON IN ROOM _____

SILLY WORD _____

NOUN _____

FIRST NAME (FEMALE) _____

NOUN _____

VERB _____

TYPE OF LIQUID _____

Adult MAD LIBS® LIFT YOUR SPIRITS

The world's greatest *food and wine* game

In my day, bars were bars, not _____ lounges for young
                                      ADJECTIVE

folks with their fancy _____. Back then, the bartender was
                              PLURAL NOUN

like a/an _____, listening to your problems _____,
              OCCUPATION   ADVERB

and giving _____ advice. The patrons were like good
                  ADJECTIVE

_____ and everybody knew your _____. In those
   PLURAL NOUN   NOUN

days, the barkeep knew how to make a stiff _____. There
                                                    NOUN

was only one kind of vodka and no silly flavors like _____.
                                                            TYPE OF FOOD

Beer was easier, too. You got a pint of whatever was on tap. Today, the

kids _____ for so-called craft beers, with names like _____'s
        VERB   PERSON IN ROOM

_____ IPA. We used to sit at the old _____ Tavern, drinking
   SILLY WORD   NOUN

our mugs and singing songs like this:

   My dear _____, my lovely _____. She left with
              FIRST NAME (FEMALE)   NOUN

   a satchel and sack. So pass the whiskey, _____ a glass,
                                                    VERB

   and pray she won't come back!

Sigh. I hear they're knocking the old place down to make room for a

coffee shop. I guess I'll have to fill my mug with _____ from
                                                          TYPE OF LIQUID

now on.

Adult MAD LIBS® YOU AND SPINACH, SITTIN' IN A TREE

The world's greatest _food and wine_ game

MAD LIBS® is fun to play with friends, but you can also play it by yourself! To begin with, DO NOT look at the story on the page below. Fill in the blanks on this page with the words called for. Then, using the words you have selected, fill in the blank spaces in the story. Now you've created your own hilarious MAD LIBS® game!

NOUN _____

ADJECTIVE _____

NUMBER _____

ANIMAL _____

PLURAL NOUN _____

NOUN _____

PLURAL NOUN _____

COLOR _____

ADJECTIVE _____

ADVERB _____

ANIMAL _____

PART OF THE BODY _____

NOUN _____

ADVERB _____

ADJECTIVE _____

ADJECTIVE _____

PERSON IN ROOM (MALE) _____

CELEBRITY _____

Adult MAD LIBS®
YOU AND SPINACH, SITTIN' IN A TREE

The world's greatest _food and wine_ game

Everybody knows that a healthy diet is the key to a long, happy

_____. If you want to live to the _____ old age
NOUN   ADJECTIVE

of _____, you can start by cutting out foods high in fat,
   NUMBER

like pizza or _____ McNuggets. Avoid salty _____
              ANIMAL   PLURAL NOUN

and sugary cereals, like Cinnamon _____ Crunch. Mom
                                  NOUN

always told you to eat your vegetables, and of course, she was right.

Visit your local farmers' market to find the freshest fruits and

_____. Remember that _____ veggies are the highest
PLURAL NOUN   COLOR

in _____ nutrients. When it comes to buying meat, choose
   ADJECTIVE

_____. A grilled _____ breast or lean _____
ADVERB   ANIMAL   PART OF THE BODY

of turkey are good choices, especially if they are _____-free
                                                   NOUN

and organic. Fish is also _____ recommended, due to its
                          ADVERB

high levels of Omega-3 _____ acids, which make your heart
                       ADJECTIVE

_____ and strong. If you follow these tips (and skip dessert)
ADJECTIVE

you can live as long as _____ Washington, and look as sexy as
                        PERSON IN ROOM (MALE)

_____!
CELEBRITY

MAD LIBS® is fun to play with friends, but you can also play it by yourself! To begin with, DO NOT look at the story on the page below. Fill in the blanks on this page with the words called for. Then, using the words you have selected, fill in the blank spaces in the story. Now you've created your own hilarious MAD LIBS® game!

NOUN _____

ADJECTIVE _____

NUMBER _____

ADVERB _____

PLURAL NOUN _____

VERB (PAST TENSE) _____

CELEBRITY _____

ADJECTIVE _____

PERSON IN ROOM (MALE) _____

TYPE OF LIQUID _____

VERB (PAST TENSE) _____

ADJECTIVE _____

ANIMAL _____

NOUN _____

ADJECTIVE _____

VERB ENDING IN "ING" _____

NOUN _____

Adult MAD LIBS® COMPLAINT LETTER

The world's greatest _food and wine_ game

Dear _____ or Madame,
NOUN

I wish to express my _____ displeasure with my meal last
ADJECTIVE

night. To begin with, your restaurant was so crowded that we had

to wait _____ minutes for our table. We were about to give
NUMBER

up and walk out when the host _____ seated us at a booth
ADVERB

next to two _____ who _____ and screamed during
PLURAL NOUN   VERB (PAST TENSE)

our entire dinner. We noticed _____ sitting across the dining
CELEBRITY

room at a very _____ table—talk about unfair! Our server,
ADJECTIVE

_____, was extremely rude, and did not even say hello
PERSON IN ROOM (MALE)

when he handed us the menu and _____ list. Throughout
TYPE OF LIQUID

the meal, he rarely _____ on us at all. When the food finally
VERB (PAST TENSE)

arrived, it was _____ at best. My companion found a/an
ADJECTIVE

_____ in her soup, and my steak had the consistency of an
ANIMAL

old _____. Even dessert left a/an _____ taste in our
NOUN   ADJECTIVE

mouths. Needless to say, we will not be _____ with you
VERB ENDING IN "ING"

again! Unless, of course, you're willing to send us a voucher for a free

_____.
NOUN

Adult MAD LIBS® OUR TRIP TO WINE COUNTRY

The world's greatest _food and wine_ game

MAD LIBS® is fun to play with friends, but you can also play it by yourself! To begin with, DO NOT look at the story on the page below. Fill in the blanks on this page with the words called for. Then, using the words you have selected, fill in the blank spaces in the story. Now you've created your own hilarious MAD LIBS® game!

PERSON IN ROOM _____

A PLACE _____

NOUN _____

NOUN _____

ADJECTIVE _____

PLURAL NOUN _____

PART OF THE BODY _____

NOUN _____

PLURAL NOUN _____

OCCUPATION _____

PLURAL NOUN _____

ADJECTIVE _____

SILLY WORD _____

ADJECTIVE _____

TYPE OF FOOD _____

VERB _____

Adult MAD LIBS® OUR TRIP TO WINE COUNTRY

The world's greatest _food and wine_ game

_____ and I have been dying to tell you about our
PERSON IN ROOM

faaaabulous wine tour in the south of (the) _____. We were
A PLACE

greeted right at the airport by our _____ guide. A friend
NOUN

of our _____ arranged for us to stay at a/an _____
NOUN   ADJECTIVE

chateau, where we were treated like royalty. From our window was

a view of rolling _____ as far as the _____ could
PLURAL NOUN   PART OF THE BODY

see. We began our trip by taking a/an _____ through the
NOUN

vineyards, and even ate some _____ off the vine. Then we
PLURAL NOUN

went inside the winery, where the _____ showed us how they
OCCUPATION

press the _____ before they're fermented. Next we saw the
PLURAL NOUN

_____ barrels where the wine is aged, or, as the French call
ADJECTIVE

it, _____. That evening, we tasted ten _____ wines,
SILLY WORD   ADJECTIVE

and paired each with a different _____. We ate and drank so
TYPE OF FOOD

much that we weren't able to _____ the next day!
VERB

Adult
MAD LIBS®
THE SECRET IS IN THE _____

The world's greatest *food and wine* game

MAD LIBS® is fun to play with friends, but you can also play it by yourself! To begin with, DO NOT look at the story on the page below. Fill in the blanks on this page with the words called for. Then, using the words you have selected, fill in the blank spaces in the story. Now you've created your own hilarious MAD LIBS® game!

PLURAL NOUN _____

ARTICLE OF CLOTHING (PLURAL) _____

EXCLAMATION _____

ADJECTIVE _____

ANIMAL _____

PART OF THE BODY _____

TYPE OF LIQUID _____

PLURAL NOUN _____

NOUN _____

NOUN _____

PLURAL NOUN _____

NOUN _____

COLOR _____

ADVERB _____

NOUN _____

ADJECTIVE _____

VERB ENDING IN "ING" _____

Adult MAD LIBS® THE SECRET IS IN THE _____

The world's greatest _food and wine_ game

When I have important _____ over for a soirée, I always
                          PLURAL NOUN

whip up my signature dish. I know it's sure to knock their

_____ off, and have them yelling "_____!" at the
ARTICLE OF CLOTHING (PLURAL)   EXCLAMATION

dinner table. To make this _____ recipe, you will need the
                              ADJECTIVE

following:

- 1 whole _____, with the _____ removed
            ANIMAL   PART OF THE BODY

- 3 cups of _____
              TYPE OF LIQUID

- 2 fresh _____, washed and peeled
            PLURAL NOUN

- 4 large eggs, beaten with a/an _____ until frothy
                                    NOUN

- 1 small container of grated _____ cheese
                                 NOUN

Season the meat with salt and _____. Put it in the
                                 PLURAL NOUN

_____ to roast at 450 degrees, until light _____. In a
NOUN   COLOR

saucepan, mix the remaining ingredients _____, occasionally
                                           ADVERB

stopping to add a pinch of _____, if needed. Pour over
                              NOUN

the dish and garnish with _____ herbs. Watch your guests
                             ADJECTIVE

_____ in delight, and congratulate yourself on a job well
VERB ENDING IN "ING"

done.

Adult MAD LIBS® THE WINE ZODIAC

The world's greatest _food and wine_ game

MAD LIBS® is fun to play with friends, but you can also play it by yourself! To begin with, DO NOT look at the story on the page below. Fill in the blanks on this page with the words called for. Then, using the words you have selected, fill in the blank spaces in the story. Now you've created your own hilarious MAD LIBS® game!

OCCUPATION (PLURAL) _____

ADJECTIVE _____

PART OF THE BODY _____

ANIMAL (PLURAL) _____

NOUN _____

ADJECTIVE _____

NOUN _____

ADJECTIVE _____

PLURAL NOUN _____

ANIMAL _____

NOUN _____

VERB ENDING IN "ING" _____

ADJECTIVE _____

You are what you eat, so the saying goes. However, a team of

_____ recently discovered that your choice of wine
OCCUPATION (PLURAL)

reveals more about your personality. For instance, Pinot Grigio

drinkers seem a little _____ at first, but once you get to
ADJECTIVE

know them, you'll realize there is more to them than meets the

_____. Sauvignon Blanc fans are social _____. They
PART OF THE BODY   ANIMAL (PLURAL)

are the kind of people you'd take to a/an _____ if you want
NOUN

to have a good time. If you go for Chardonnay, you are assertive and

_____-hearted. If you drink Moscato, you are as sweet as
ADJECTIVE

a/an _____. People feel _____ when you are around.
NOUN   ADJECTIVE

Pinot Noir lovers are romantic _____. They exude the grace
PLURAL NOUN

of a/an _____, and the mystery of a/an _____.
ANIMAL   NOUN

Cabernet Sauvignon aficionado? You are dominant and used to

_____ your way. And beware of Shiraz groupies. They are the
VERB ENDING IN "ING"

_____ kids who will get you into trouble. The next time you
ADJECTIVE

meet someone, don't ask what their sign is—find out what they drink

instead!

Download Mad Libs today!

Join the millions of Mad Libs fans creating
wacky and wonderful stories on our apps!